COLOR AND LEARN

Learning about music is fun. This book combines music signs and symbols with familiar objects, designed to capture the interest of the pre-school child.

Talk about the pictures and relate them to music. Help the child Color and Learn.

Layout/Illustration: Jeannette Aquino
Editor: Carole Flatau
Production: Frank J. Hackinson

TREBLE CLEF SIGN

This means high

Color the Treble Clef Si

This is a MUSICAL STAFF

Color the lines blue

Color the spaces yellow

THE MUSICAL ALPHABET

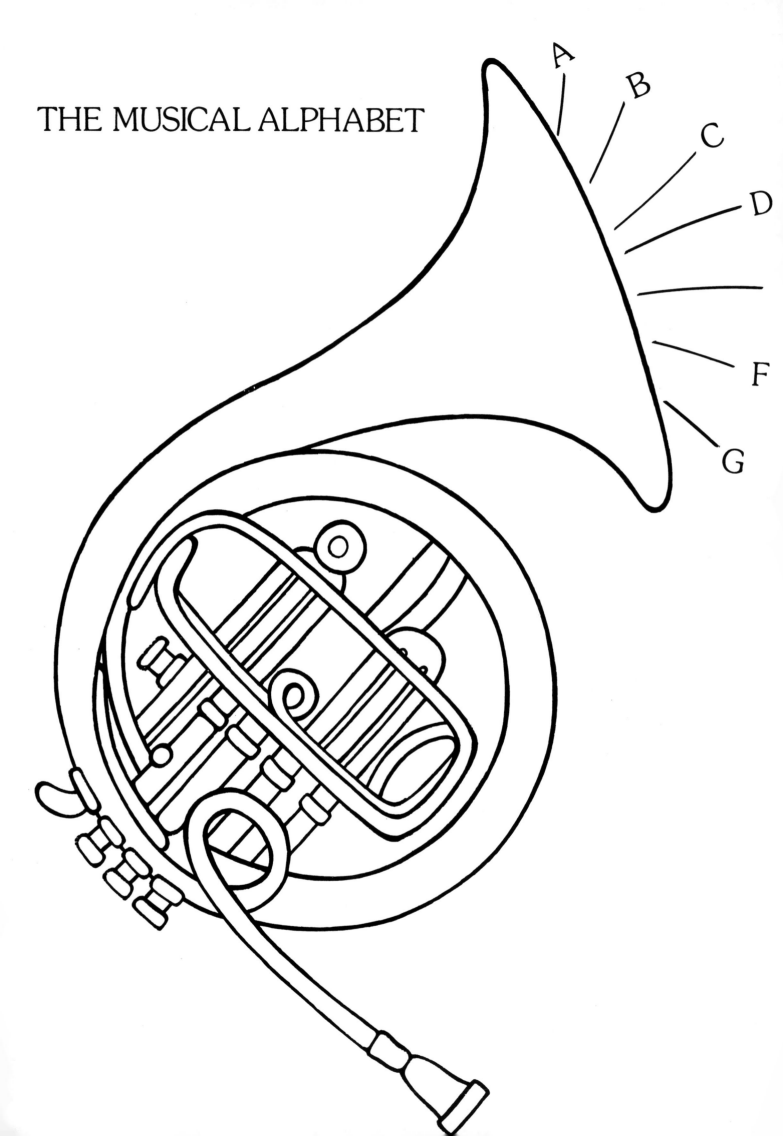

THE MUSICAL ALPHABET

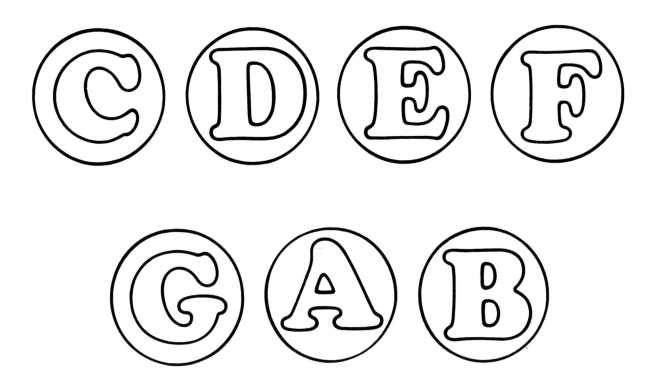

Color the letters in the Musical Alphabet

This is MIDDLE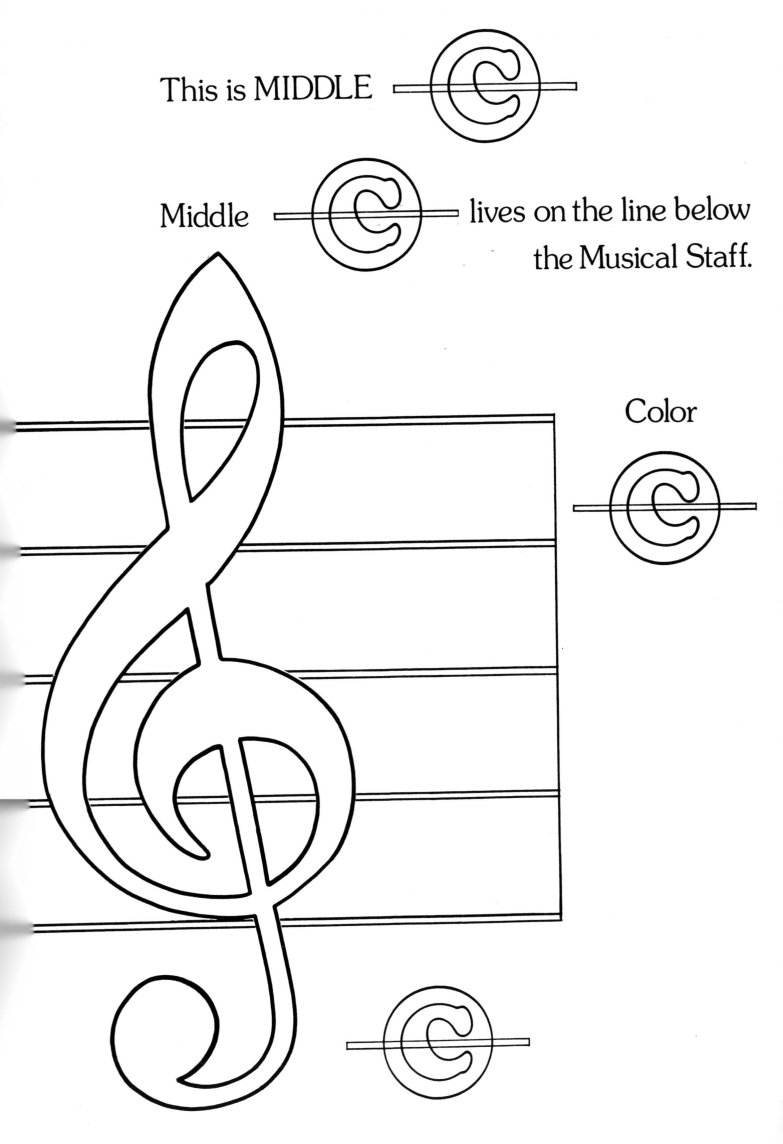

Middle ━━ lives on the line below the Musical Staff.

Color

This is  lives in the first space of the Musical Staff.

Color

MUSICAL NOTES

Color the Musical Notes

REST-SH

Color the Rest Signs

Rest means "sh"

UP

Color the Sharp Signs

Sharp means up

DOWN

Color the Flat Signs

Flat means down

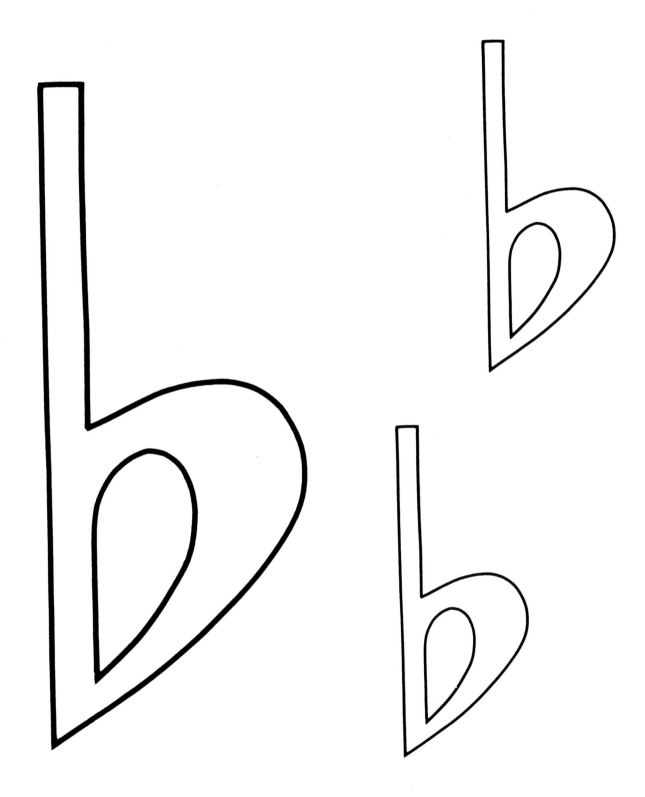

TIME STUDY

TIME STUDY

Color the Musical Notes

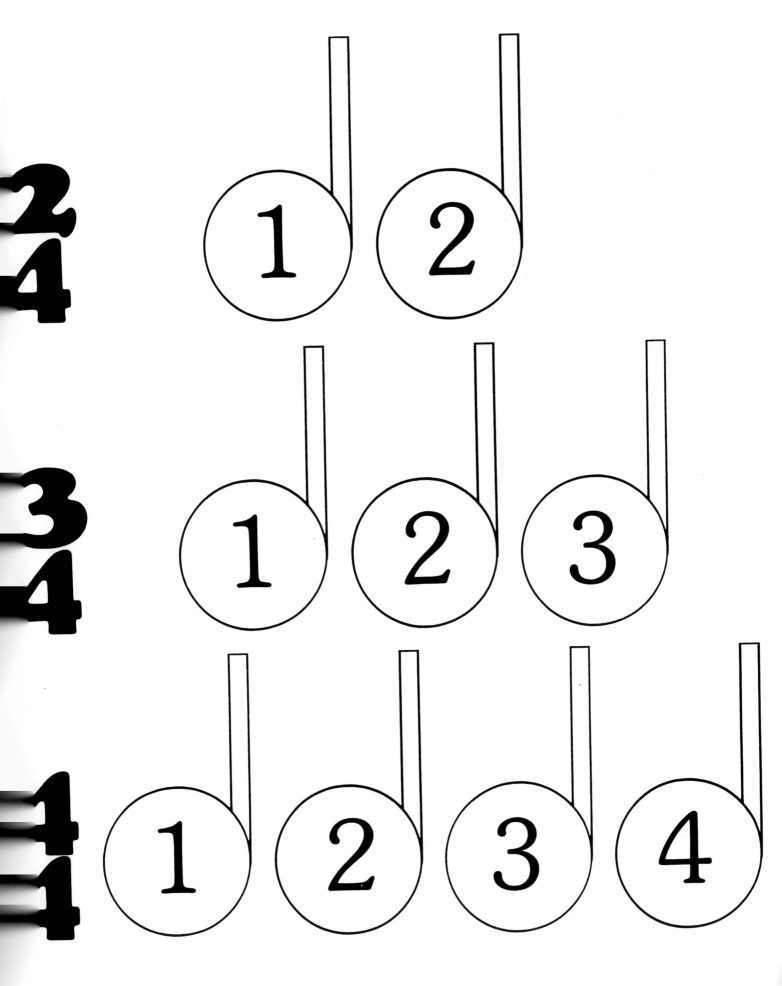

MUSIC FUN
Clap hands on the notes
"sh" on the rests

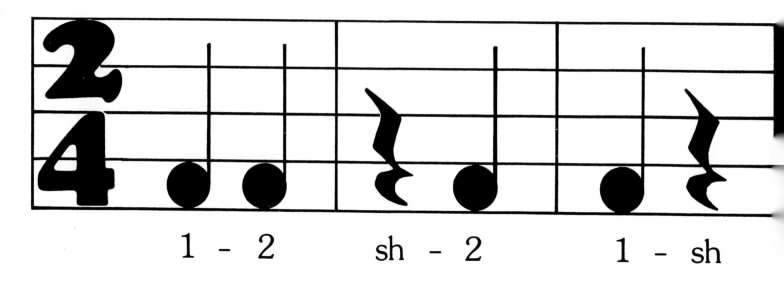

| 1 - 2 | sh - 2 | 1 - sh |

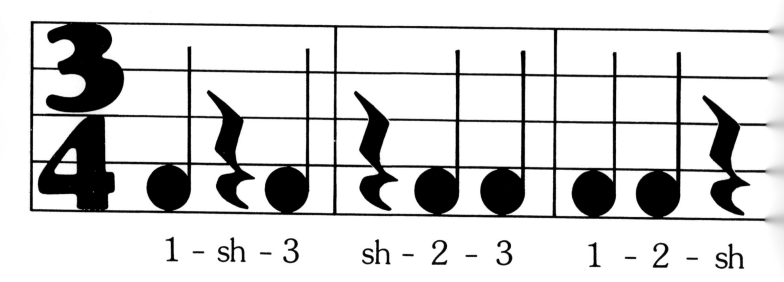

| 1 - sh - 3 | sh - 2 - 3 | 1 - 2 - sh |

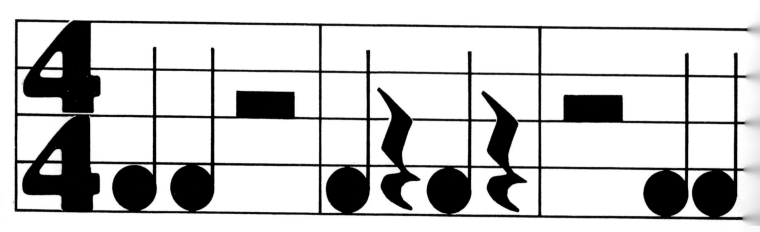

| 1 - 2 -sh-sh | 1 - sh - 2 -sh | sh-sh - 3 - 4 |

COLOR AND CUT OUT

TREBLE CLEF SIGN

Treble means high.

Put him on the Musical Staff.

COLOR AND CUT OUT

TREBLE CLEF SIGN

Treble means high.

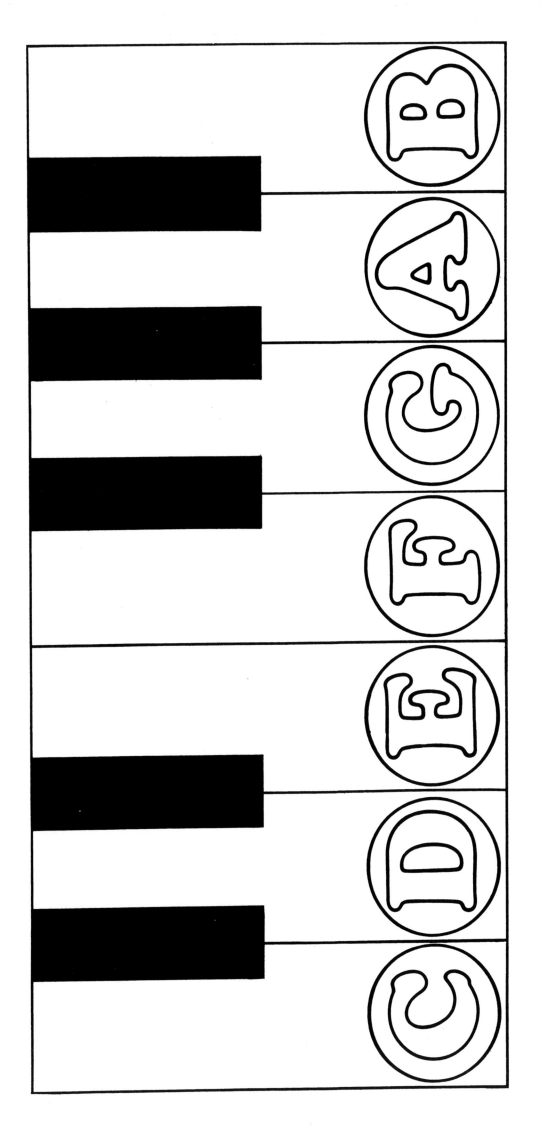

This is a PIANO KEYBOARD.

Cut out your Musical Alphabet and put them on the Keyboard.

USICAL STAFF

PHABET IN THEIR HOUSES

EF SIGN ON THE STAFF

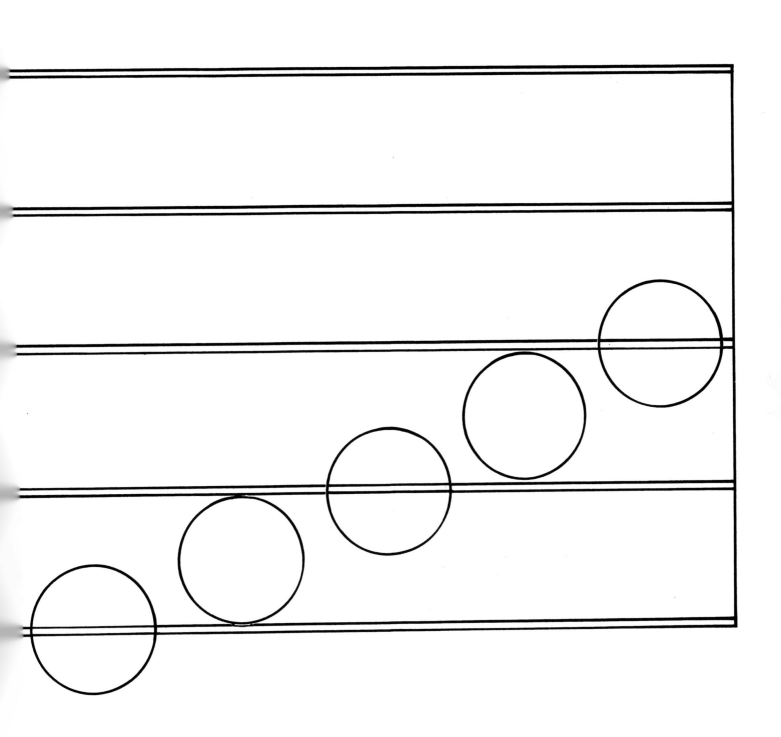

THE PIANO KEYBOARD

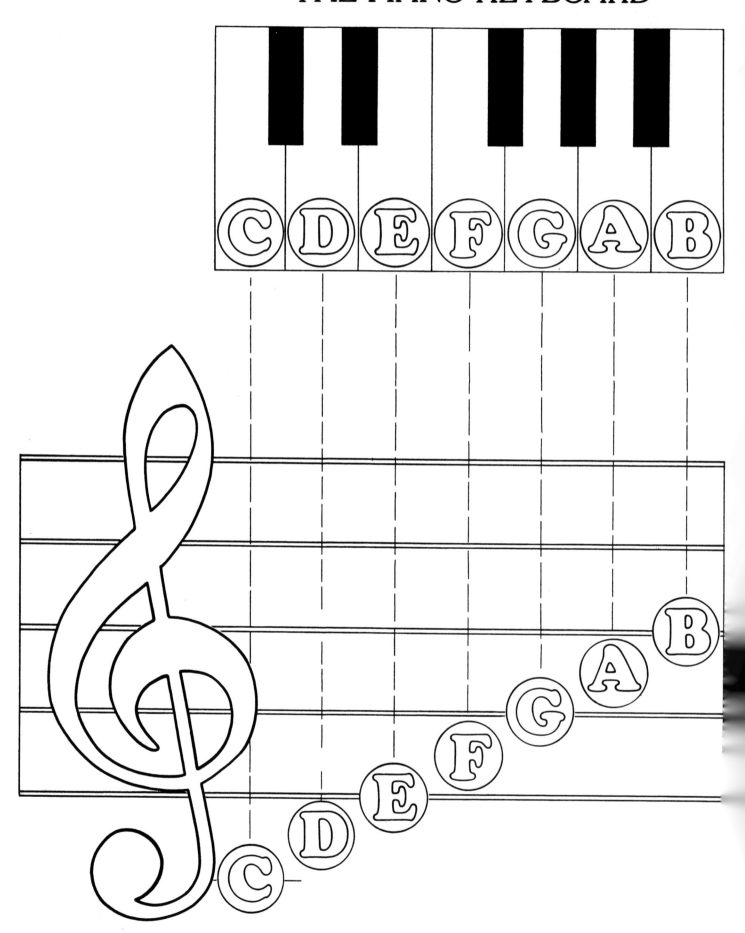

THE MUSICAL STAFF

NOW
WE
PLAY

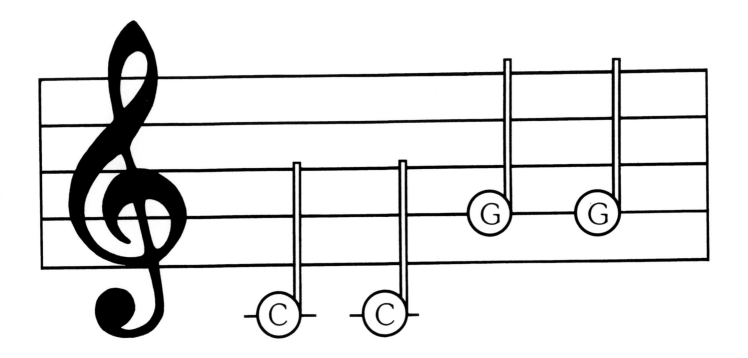

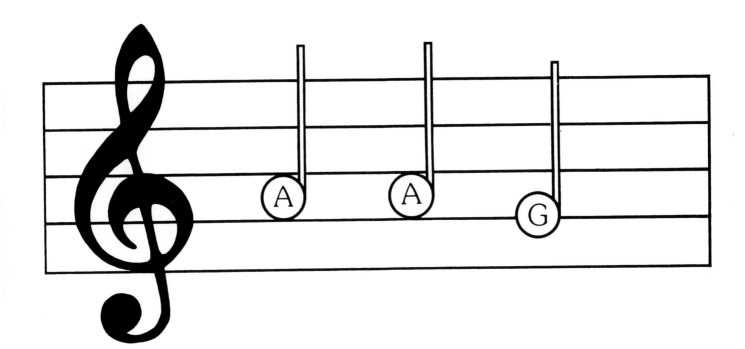

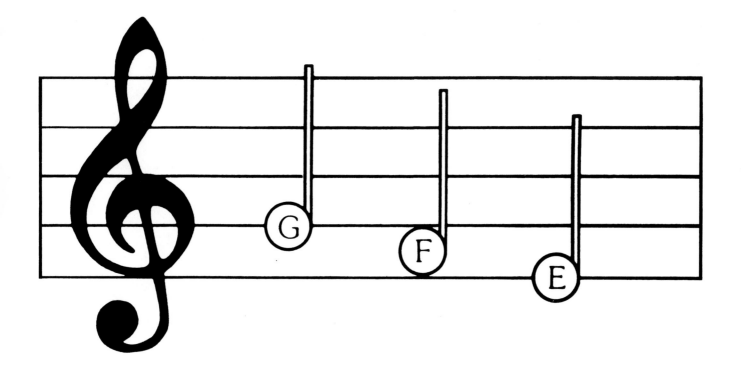

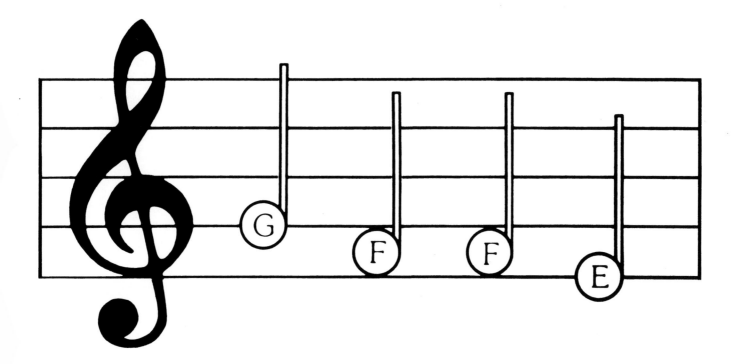

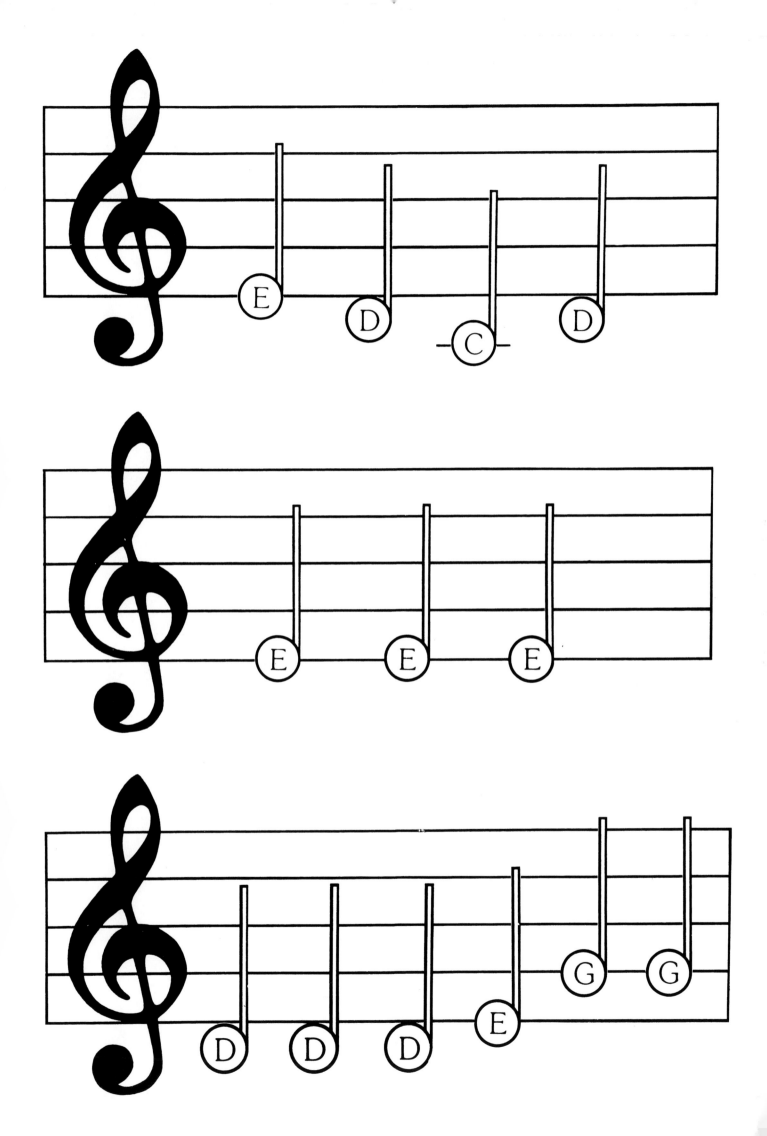

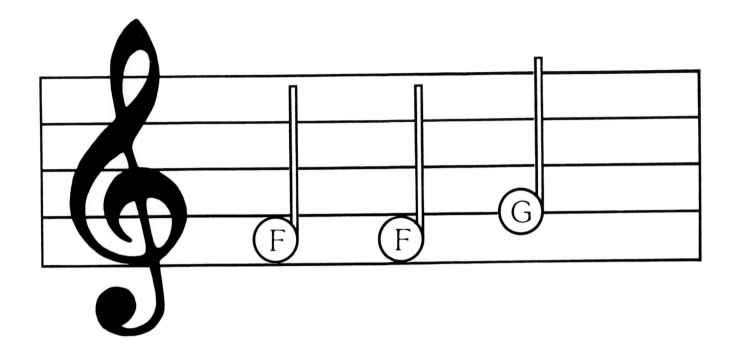

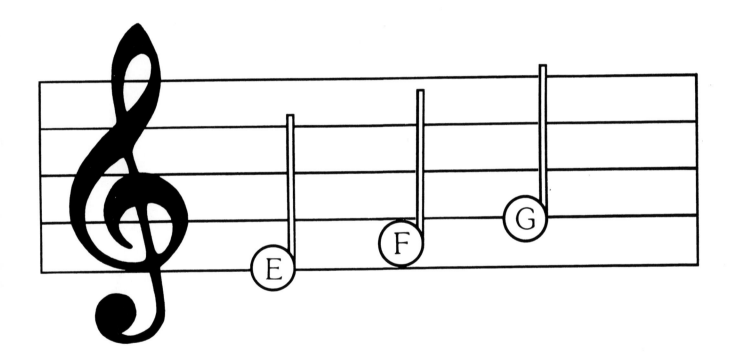

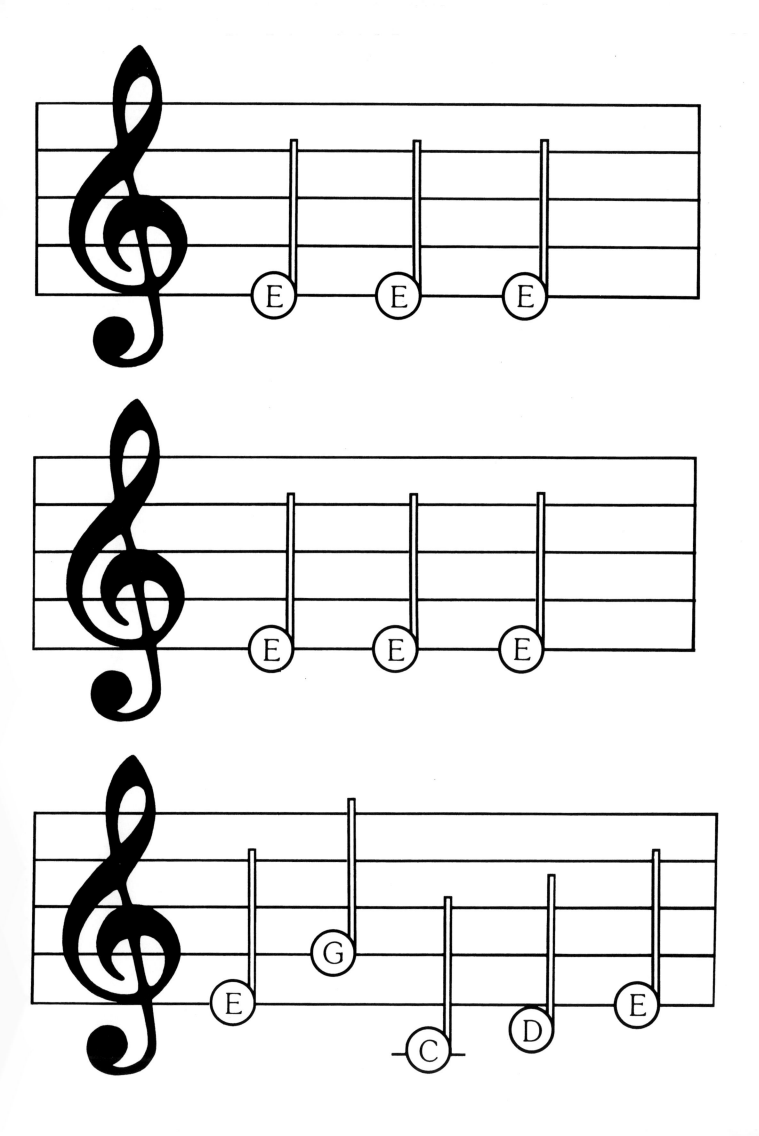